# DRAFT BOARD BLUES

Robert Cooperman

FUTURECYCLE PRESS

*www.futurecycle.org*

Library of Congress Control Number: 2017938698

Published by FutureCycle Press
Athens, Georgia, USA

ISBN 978-1-942371-27-4

*My thanks to Bill Brennan, John Vance and Earle Wescott
for invaluable information and, even more, for their great stories
and, most of all, for their friendship.*

*In memory of Mark Gross, a good man in a bad war.*

*As always, this book is for my beloved Beth.*

# CONTENTS

## PART III.
## WAR BUSINESS

## PART IV.
## "I DECLARE THE WAR IS OVER."

## DRAFT BOARD BLUES

I got the draft board blues,
I'm as blue as blue can be.
I got the draft board blues,
The army's comin' after me.

They won't be happy
'Til I'm in the ground;
If they see me standin'
They'll shove me six feet down,
'Cause I'm just the hare
And they're the big ole hound.
I got the draft board blues.

I got the draft board blues,
I gotta get right outta here.
I got the draft board blues,
Please hide me, anywhere.

If the VC don't get me
Then the Army will.
That's why I'm poppin'
All these goof-ball pills
And tryin' to make myself
Look deathly ill.
I got the draft board blues.

I got the draft board blues,
Got no beef with Mr. Minh;
I got the draft board blues,
For all I know he's next of kin.

We're just proppin' up
A corrupt regime,
And I heard there's lots of oil,
And that's our real scheme:
To suck it all up,
Leave Vietnam stripped clean.
I got the draft board blues.

I got the draft board blues,
The army's screamin' dominoes;
I got the draft board blues,
Every country's gonna go.
First Laos, then Thailand,
Then old Cambodia,
Indonesia's next to fall,
And great big India
With a billion more Commies
Who'll breathe up all our air,
Then they'll be movin' in,
Right over here,
And if you believe that one,
I got a bridge for you, I swear.

I got the draft board blues.

# PART I.
## 1-A

"Sarge, I'm only eighteen, I got a ruptured spleen
and I always carry a purse."

—Phil Ochs, "Draft Dodger Rag"

## MY DRAFT CARD

1964, right before Vietnam started to rage
like a picador-tormented bull, but young enough
for draft cards to mean only I was legal to buy alcohol:
adulthood conferred in that paper rectangle.

So, with a friend in a neighborhood liquor store,
I bought a pint of scotch and a bottle of raspberry soda,
a concoction so sickeningly ignorant, the owner should've
warned us, but figured it was our funeral, and it was.

Somehow, we stumbled onto a churchyard stone bench—
no idea how we got there—warmed ourselves
with the vile potion that tasted better with each swig,
and yowled folksongs about heartless women,
until someone in the looming apartment house
thrust Medusa-wild hair out her window and shouted,

"Shut up, some of us got to work in the morning!"

Somehow, I staggered to the subway, rode
that earthquake home to the inevitable eruption:
my mother bemoaning she'd raised a drunkard.

But I hadn't a thought about what that draft card—
pawing my wallet as if taunted by a red cape—meant.

## "FEEL LIKE I'M FIXIN' TO DIE RAG"

While Vietnam blared its deadly
tympani and off-key, raging bagpipes,
we sang along with Country Joe's,
"Well, it's one, two, three,
what are we fighting for?"

Like Joe, none of us had a clue,
knew only that before
we'd be lemminged into death-
dripping jungles, we'd be damned
to a hell worse than any Dante
could rhyme on with the glee of a man
who truly believed in getting even.

We were kids with our whole lives
ahead of us, and, if necessary, could starve,
eat, or crazy our way out of getting killed.

Except Peter, who played guitar
and sang, when we sat and cursed
the war, the army, and the draft.

Peter refused to scheme his way out,
saying, "It's only a two-year hitch,"
with such innocence I hit him.
He took no offense, just added,
while he flicked off a lovely riff,
"You'll see, I'll be out in no time."

"No time" was exactly what he had:
stepping on a claymore within a week,
the music that mine made nothing
like the notes he coaxed from his guitar.

## HAD I BEEN CALLED

Had I been called to serve in World War II,
I'd like to think I'd have gone without
a whimper, at least not one out loud,
and been shipped out to Europe or Asia,
and pissed and shat myself: a coward,
but impossible not to fight in that war.

Most likely I'd have died, on D-Day,
at the Bulge, on a nameless Pacific island,
a French, Belgian, or German farmyard:
from a sniper's bullet while resting after a march
or a battle in which I'd mostly ducked and cringed.
I hope I wouldn't have been killed running away
or begging for my life, or abandoning a buddy,
and that it would've been over in an instant.

But Vietnam? The lie that generals and Congress
and LBJ, then Nixon, told us was to save
our glorious democracy; and if we believed that one,
they could sell us some prime real estate on Mars.

No thanks, not for me, my brother, my friends,
not for anyone, though enough boys did go
that by the end they had to build a long black wall
to hold all the names of all the kids butchered
in jungle mud, and they called that wall, "Art,"
and all of it was for nothing, for nothing.

## WHO WENT AND WHO DIDN'T

Let's be honest,
if you were a rich
and powerful man's son
you didn't have to go in
unless you wanted to get away
from the blowhard,
or felt a duty to serve,
or thought
that as a war hero
you'd win political office.

If you were white, middle-class,
a city or suburban boy,
there were doctors' notes
diagnosing you were afflicted
by any number of lethal diseases;
shrinks' letters lamenting
you were a dope fiend,
a homosexual, crazier
than a birthday balloon,
air zooming out of it.

There were student deferments,
and maybe the war would end
before the diploma was rammed
into your terrified hand.
There were teaching jobs,
conscientious objector status,
or—if you were truly desperate—
Canada, Sweden, if you brought
enough money, so you weren't
a parasite-hippie.

But God forbid
you were from a small town,
a farm, were black or Latino,
or all of the above,
and your family needed
the combat pay, or worse,
a judge roared,

"Prison or the army,"
so off you went,
like a British convict
transported to the Antipodes.

And if you weren't lucky,
shipped home in a box,
or without some limbs,
or maybe in one piece
but you couldn't sleep,
you drank, did drugs,
had flashbacks of fire fights,
of buddies dying in your arms,

and no one understood why
you couldn't just get on with your life,
instead of fighting with your family,
your girlfriend, your wife,
who might finally sob
she and the kids were afraid of you.

So maybe you'd end up
on the street, hearing voices,
the VA swearing nothing was wrong,
and you really, really wanted
to believe that, but knew
you were twisted up inside,
and no way you could ever
get straightened out again.

## 1969

"$19.69," the clerk informs me,
as my pen hovers above my checkbook.
"1969," he murmurs.

"A pretty good year for music,
unless you were stuck in Vietnam,"
to which sentiment I agree,
recalling the spider web
of my local draft board.

I don't look back
with nostalgia to that year,
only relief that I survived it
and 1970 and '71.

Indeed, until that postal clerk
mentioned it, I hadn't
thought of 1969 in decades,

and as for the music
that made us crazy, delirious,
that lifted us almost to heaven,

I'd gladly never have heard it
if it meant the army
hadn't stalked me
and everyone I knew:
the draft board,
our personal serial killer.

## COMING OF AGE DURING THE VIETNAM WAR

A week before my physical, I sat
on a night-cold bench and smoked a joint,
tired of staring at my four walls, of feeling
sorry for myself and none of the women I knew
offering to come over and assuage my terror.

But paranoia of the dark, the dread of next week
began to call out like huge night predators.
So I stood, as the world teetered like a top
overwhelmed by the entropy that will get us all,
and shuffled toward my apartment: too cold,
with a bullwhip of snow lashing the air,
for the old Puerto Rican men to play dominoes
on the sidewalk and keep Union Street safe.

Almost at my door, I was accosted by a cop
backing me against his shark-sleek black-and-white,
demanding why I was swerving like a flea.

"Officer," I spat, "if I can be blown to hell
for my country, I can get stoned tonight,"
and cringed at the expected blow, his slapping
on the cuffs, ramming me into the backseat.

Instead, he asked if I needed help home;
when I pointed I was home, he murmured,

"Be careful, kid, it's a dangerous world."

## AUGUST 18, 1957

A morning of late August heat,
three of us horsing around outside
our apartment house, two against me.
I ran, and since eleven-year-old boys
are cursorial creatures, they gave
predator-chase while I circled back,
laughing, to escape into the building.
But when I hit the lobby door,
the pane of etched glass gave:
my blood, whale-spume;
luckily, a doctor across the street.

That was long ago, and I'm still here,
in case anyone has any silly ideas,
which is what I showed a bigger kid
who thought me an easy mark,
until I unwrapped the dressing
and shoved the witch-pus-y wound
into his face; he screamed,
a guy with more grease in his hair
than a Corvette's engine,
who wore his smokes wrapped
in his T-shirt sleeve, his biceps
bulging as if he pumped iron
every twenty minutes.

## PHYSICAL, FORT HAMILTON

The thing of it was, I really
did believe I had a legitimate out:
When I was eleven, I'd crashed
through a glass door while playing
with friends, the pane shattered,
and so many arteries and veins severed,
it was like splicing a rattler's nest
of wires to sew them all together,
and if the doctor hadn't lived next door,
the army never would've had a chance
to get its claws into me.

My right hand had less feeling
than a salami; it never grew a millimeter,
was stiff as a manual-stick shift
in sub-zero cold.

So at Station Eleven—where all of us
with physical or mental complaints
were herded for one last chance
to prove ourselves unfit—I showed
the doctor my scars, my hand,
my physician's letter.

He held out a magic-trick dime
and told me to pick it up,

"With your left hand," slapping
the bad one away like a fly.

## THE APTITUDE TEST: FORT HAMILTON

Marched into a classroom,
we were handed tests, a sergeant bellowing,

"If you mens think y'all can get
every question wrong and that'll prove
you're too stupid to serve your country,
think again. No one fails; the worse you do,
the quicker y'all go to Vietnam. Begin!"

The first section: synonyms, antonyms,
such and such word is to something
or other as this other word is to what?
I blasted through. The second section,
arithmetic for idiot fourth graders.

Then the third: illustrations of tools
and four choices about their use;
I was adrift on a sea of ignorance:
my one experience with a nail
was to accidentally sit on one,
a tetanus shot rammed into my tush.
I identified hammer and screwdriver;
the rest, arcane implements of torture.

Diabolically last, a series of flat planes;
we had to tell what three-dimensional figure
they'd end up as: impossible origami.
I guessed and guessed, and hoped, prayed
if I had to go in, I'd be made a clerk,
but trembled I was battle-bound.

## IN SOME FAMILIES

In some families,
there's a tradition
of serving in the military.

In mine, my father epiphanied
that World War II was ending
and he had a family to start;
plus, I knew Vietnam was as evil
as Satan cackling to harvest boys
who really did believe
that if they didn't defend America
in a far-off jungle, we'd all
be slaughtered in our beds.

When Dad saw me, quaking
like a field mouse at the letter
for my army physical, he asked,

"Do you want to serve?"
My mouth too dry to speak,
I shook my head like a horse failing
to rid itself of the steel bit.
"Okay then," he nodded,
as if he had some plan
that was so secret
he couldn't divulge it
even to me.

## *THE GREEN BERETS*, STARRING JOHN WAYNE

Wayne was silver-screen courageous in Vietnam,
when, during World War II, as a young man,
he protected the home front by making movies,
while my uncle fought through Italy, France,
Germany, the air a blizzard of shells.
And as for that Commie-novelist Dashiell Hammett,
at age 48 he volunteered to fight the Nazis,
the Japanese, but deemed too old for combat,
he was shipped to a post in Alaska,
to monitor radio transmissions.

But Wayne wasn't the only super-patriot
who thundered it was my duty to fight and die:
George Jessel, the hoofer-comedian, spat
that any kid who didn't sign up was a coward.
Martha Rae, the ancient comedienne,
would wear Edith Head-tailored uniforms
and salute the flag, her feral eyes darting
like a wildcat whenever she marched
in place on TV specials.

Not last, Kate Smith, the sentimental vocalist-
anti-Semite extraordinaire, who belted out
"God Bless America," as if only she
were patriotic enough to sing it,
the rest of us expected to stand,
place hands over hearts, then enlist
the instant she finished.

If we didn't, we could all go to hell;
she'd be only too happy to send us there.

## ON RELIGIOUS GROUNDS

In our last year of college deferments,
all of us hearing the time-bomb ticking,
feeling the wind of the blade swinging,
even while we sat, one evening, playing
poker, smoking dope, I asked a friend
his plan to evade the bayonet of Vietnam.

"Religious grounds," Ace declared,
a face straight as five to the king.

"But you're an atheist," I objected,
ever his inadvertent straight man.

"Not so! I'm a man of great faith.
A devout coward," to crack us all up:
not hard, considering the flags of smoke
shooting from our lungs and how scared
we were trying not to show each other
and ourselves we were.

In the end, Ace scored a draft number
more bullet-proof than a royal flush.
Free, he went to Israel, married,
served in the IDF and died
in the Yom Kippur War, caught
holding the fifth ace of a true believer.

## AN URBAN LEGEND ABOUT THE ARMY PHYSICAL

It was always some guy hearing,
swearing that this had been done
by someone else, that he had it
on good authority it was a more
sure-fire method of getting out
than being born hydrocephalic.

To wit, a guy spread—but maybe
you won't want to read further—
peanut butter all over his anus,
so when he bent and exposed his cheeks
to the army doctor to examine
for what they once called, "Piles,"
the quack was presented
with what looked like...

Well I don't want to think about
what it looked like, but alleged to be
the surest sign you were so nuts,
or so physically ill, the army wanted
less to do with you than with a battalion
of Black Panthers learning to violently
overthrow the government.

No one I knew ever confessed to,
or bragged about, smudging brown
desperation, to save his arse—forgive
the pun—from being blown off,
so who knows if it's true:
truth, as we all know, having less
to do with facts than with what
we need to believe.

## THANKSGIVING DINNER: MY UNCLE'S HOUSE

The army's invitation to fire an M-16,
toss grenades, and jab a bayonet
wouldn't arrive for another month or so,
though I sensed the letter's approach:
collecting the mail in shaking-hand dread.

The whole family was driving to New Bedford
for Thanksgiving dinner, and my Aunt Grace's
legendary Sephardic style turkey: basted
in raisins and a spicy olive oil-tomato sauce.

This year, my uncle's World War II buddies
sat drinking scotch in Uncle Sid's den,
all shaking their heads at the Vietcong and how,
"Those dirty little bastards don't fight fair."

Maybe it was the scotch I hadn't puked up,
or knowing the army's letter was winging
toward me like dragon-doom; but I exploded:
"Fighting fair? Like we do? Interrogating
anyone who looks like the enemy, then shoving them
out of helicopters into the Gulf of Tonkin,
hitting the water like slabs of concrete!"

Uncle Sid told me to mind my manners.
In his eyes I was now a coward and a traitor,
though he still loved me, even if it would be his sad
duty to snap my neck, as he'd done to Nazis
for the good of our country, and for my eternal
salvation, which we Jews didn't really believe in.

## SUPER BOWL III, JANUARY 12, 1969

Our Jets against the Baltimore Colts,
the game we'd waited for all our underdog lives.
When I'd opened the mail the day before,
there was what I'd dreaded for months
after the physical that I'd protested
had been handled with the incompetence
of Daffy Duck: the army's invitation to join
their Vietnam adventure, two weeks, then I'd report,
the clock ticking faster than the descending blade
in a Poe story set in a madman's dungeon.

I felt like watching a football game as much
as I wanted to attend my own funeral,
but my friends insisted:

"It'll cheer you up," Paul promised.
"We'll order out deli, smoke reefer, drink beer,
and maybe the Jets won't lose too badly,"
though Broadway Joe Namath had guaranteed
a win, the beloved chutzpah of all New Yorkers.

The pastrami on rye hit my stomach
in crimson, greasy strips on cardboard,
and despite the Jets' lead, I staggered to the bathroom,
not even the excuse of being as drunk
as a concussed kick-returner.

Washing my face, gargling cold water,
I made my way out: final score, Jets, 16-7,
Paul thumping me on the back, swearing
that anything was possible.

## THE PARTY

Two nights before I was to report
to Fort Hamilton and train to kill or die
in Vietnam, my friends threw me a party.

One tried to convince me to leave for
Canada or Sweden—oh, I was tempted—
another gave me an acid tab he boasted
was spiked with "something outrageous"
and told me to pop it an hour before
"You take the oath" and let it do the rest;
another flashed a Bowie blade
and offered to cleave off
my offending trigger finger.

"The army can't be any crazier,"
I muttered, but knew I was wrong
and sat on the couch, slugging beers,
smoking joint after joint, the hours ticking
in my head like the clock inside
the crocodile stalking Captain Hook.

Then Belinda—Paul's granny-dressed
pre-Raphaelite girlfriend—sat down
and kissed and kissed me, telling me
this was her going-away gift.

"So you'll remember me,"
as if anyone could forget Belinda.

## THE BLANK CHECK

At my going-away party,
Frank handed me a blank check.

"Go to Canada, Sweden,"
he pleaded, "anywhere but
that meat grinder,"
almost as afraid
for me as I was.

I didn't have the courage;
easier to serve and die.
Frank sighed, hugged me,
and stuck the check
into my shirt pocket,

"In case you change your mind,"
then, no heart to stick around,
he pivoted smart as a corporal
on parade and strode out.

After everyone had left,
I stared at his check,
as if a verse by Nostradamus
foretelling my obvious future,
then tore it into
a thousand little pieces.

## AT THE INDUCTION CENTER: FORT HAMILTON, BROOKLYN

My parents dropped me off
in the dark winter false dawn.
We hugged, not wanting to admit
we might never see each other again.

"You'll be back," Dad cuffed my chin.
"Be safe," Mom fluted, through tears.

They drove away, my mother waving,
battlefield-smoke exhaust fumes lingering;
I trudged toward the gym, my heart
so skittish I feared, hoped, I'd die
before the army had a chance to drag out
my torment, then kill me in the jungle.

"Okay, you mens," a sergeant stood
like a fat colossus at the center,
drawling my worst nightmares
of a Klan lynching.
"When your name's called,
step forward to take the oath!"

I closed my eyes through the As,
the first of the Bs; then, another voice:
"Copperman!" Could he mean me?
"Copperman, God damnit!
Raise your fucking hand,
Robert Goddamn Copperman!"

"I think, Sir," I squeaked,
"you mean 'Cooperman,' Sir."

"Whatever, girlie, fall out
for another physical,
you're not going in today."

## THE SECOND PHYSICAL: FORT HAMILTON

This time, to see if I could pick up
a dime with my broom handle-stiff
right hand, not the healthy left one
the doctor had pointed to the first time.
Now, he examined the stricken hand,
fingers rigid as a dead sparrow's talons;
as little feeling as a kicked rock.

He told me to look away, then jabbed
the hand with a needle: not a blink;
he examined the fingers again,
murmured how small the hand was
compared to the other one
I could palm a basketball with.

He told me to pick up the fateful dime
and let me try with my right hand,
the coin skidding away like a cockroach.

"Okay," he said, and I hoped he'd let me
go home for the rest of my relieved life;
but again he told me to use my left hand.

"You can always fire with that one, son,"
he reassured me, afraid I'd have been crushed
not to be shipped off to Vietnam.
Still, I'd had a brief reprieve, a glimpse,
a whiff of freedom with that second physical.

"Screw you!" I muttered as I walked
into cold morning light. "I'll die outright,
before I'll let you kill me in your bullshit war."

# PART II.
# THE SHRINK'S LETTER

"Besides, I ain't no fool, I'm going to school,
And I'm working in a defense plant."

—Phil Ochs, "Draft Dodger Rag"

## THE SHRINK'S LETTER

How my dad knew him I'd not a clue,
but the shrink asked me questions
and wrote down every lie I almost believed:
that I had nightmares about Vietnam—
that one was true: sitting raccoon-rimmed
and sleepless-eyed on his deep leather sofa—
while I chanted my fears of jungle death,
of being singled out for special torture by NCOs:
forced to run in circles, shrieking,

"I am a shit bird!" while dodging fired rounds,
then ordered countless push-ups, then beaten
by every other draftee for being a Jew,
a college boy, a New Yorker;
for wanting to fuck my cousin Roy—
who didn't exist—after his sister Sarah—
who I'd made up too, with her cantaloupe tits—
sucked me off, then cheered me on;
worse, for bogarting oxygen meant for patriots
gung-ho to fight and kill and die
for our best-ever Jesus-loving democracy.

At the end of the session, he capped
his fountain pen as if he'd heard it all before,
and much worse, and said he'd mail me
and my draft board copies of the letter;
I placed the fee on his desk, cash only.

## HOW MY COUSIN GOT OUT

Before the army could invite him
to join all the fun in Vietnam,
Myron enrolled in rabbinical school,
was ordained and sent to a small
congregation in a St. Louis suburb.

Before he left, he confided being terrified
of Vietnam, of dying in the mud, crying
for Aunt Jean to tell him he'd be fine.
I nodded, the same fear gripping me
like a hand from my grave
when I thought about the War.

"I could've volunteered," he sighed,
"as an army chaplain in-country.
But I took the coward's way out."

He wanted me to assure him the war
was obscene; that it was worse than foolish
to go to that killing ground. I did,
telling myself the same about my attempts
to elude the draft: an exhausted fox
cornered by a pack of hounds.

Myron always attended shul, knew all
the prayers. "Mostly," he said, "because
the tunes are beautiful and sad as hell."

He smiled, took another toke, and handed
back the joint as we sat on a park bench,
his parents proud he'd carry on the faith,
relieved he wouldn't be in a combat zone.

"At least," Myron tried to joke over the roach,
"you'll get righteous weed in Nam."
I exhaled a thick flag of smoke.

## SITTING SHIVA WITH THE ROSENS

Though I lived on the other side of Brooklyn,
it was no secret in my parents' apartment house
that I'd have sold my soul to escape Vietnam.

Most tenants, even the men who'd served
in World War II and Korea, could care less
than they did about Khrushchev's breakfast.

Not Mrs. Rosen, whose son Ritchie volunteered;
she was prouder than if he played Carnegie Hall.
Whenever I'd visit my parents, she'd shout,

"There's the coward! There's the traitor!"

Then the shattering news: a landmine,
Ritchie bled out like a wrung sponge.
My mother insisted we sit shiva with the family.

"Mrs. Rosen won't want me in her apartment,"
I sighed, but resigned myself to her spitting in my face.
Instead, she steered me to a private corner.

"Whatever it takes," she growled. "Canada, Sweden,
fake being crazy. Ritchie was enough, too much.
I can't bear another boy dying for those bastards."

## HOW THEY GOT OUT

Paul ignored the doctor at the physical,
who warned his blood pressure
had to be lowered, and gave him six months
of a 1-Y deferment to reduce the numbers
below the speed of escape velocity.
Instead, he ate enough bacon and eggs
to make pigs and chickens believe
they hadn't died in vain.

Simon, thin as a guitar string, was told
to get his weight up: his blood pressure
so dangerously low you might think him
dead already; he subsisted on one meal
a day so meager Devil's Island prisoners,
out of pity, might've shared their rations.

Finally, Peter, who'd spent his life
on a shrink's couch spitting rage at his father,
a man warm as a snapping turtle
with far less affection for his only son,
who could barely stand to be in the same room
with more than three people, and stuttered
like a pinball machine blinking in tilt.
His psychiatrist's letter got him
the precious-as-a-ruby 4-F, which meant,
"Son, we don't ever want to see you again."

Then there was Ritchie Rosen,
who got out by being sent home
in a box no one had the courage to open,
and buried in New York's Montefiore Cemetery:
his parents politely telling the sergeant,
who asked if they'd prefer Arlington,
to take a flying leap back to Vietnam.

## AT THE DRAFT BOARD, I

The waiting room smelled of fear,
of damp trouser-legs, where hands
had tried to dry and calm themselves,
while the secretary bullied papers
into rigid piles; draft-age boys terrified,
paralyzed beneath her dragon-glare accusing,

"Conscientious Objector? A real one
would stride into battle unarmed
and let the enemy use him for target practice
while his comrades waited for the Vietcong
to celebrate, so our glorious warriors
could ambush that band of gutless Commies."

Or, in my case, "Too crazy to serve?
Too crazy not to, you phony 4-F liar!"

When I arrived early to be grilled by the men
who'd determine if I'd die in war or be spared
that honor, the secretary—with her helmet
of blue hair and her bosom that could crush
an infant—was nowhere to be seen.

So, daring as a spy, I examined my file:
my shrink's letter hidden at the bottom;
quick as cat-burglar-Cary-Grant, I shifted
the letter to the top and sat back down.

When the secretary returned from the Ladies',
or from visiting her father, Satan, in Hell,
and shot me a sneer of, "Abandon hope,"
I tried to look even dumber than she thought me.

## AT THE DRAFT BOARD, II

I was scolded into the room where four men waited.
Less terrified, I might've seen how tired they were,
how much they wanted to be home, relaxing,
not doing the pitiless task of deciding whether boys
the age of their sons should be sent to war, or reprieved:

whether our psychiatric or Conscientious Objector
appeals should be granted, and best-case scenario
for cowards like me—who'd applied for both—
told that the army wanted no part of me
and I was free from the killing, the dying,
the screaming prayers to our mothers to please,
please make the pain and terror go away.

Three men grilled me about why I deserved
to be a conscientious objector, the fourth read
my shrink's letter, turned one single-spaced page
face down after another, deliberate as a judge
studying complex, contradictory evidence.

"You're a traitor, aren't you?" one shouted,
"nothing but a goddamn, yellow traitor!"
The other two picked up the accusation's scent,
my mouth drier than if I were swamp-pursued
by a pack of hounds; finally, the fourth hissed,

"Go easy on this kid; I think he's nuts."
The others suddenly asked if I needed
a couple of aspirins, a cup of water, hot tea?
When I shook my head, they ushered me out;
the secretary scowled, an owl that's missed its kill.

## ANOTHER MEANS OF ESCAPE

One friend who went in
eluded the tiger trap of Vietnam:
he could type, so he was made company clerk,
and when the golden memo alit
on his desk like Noah's dove of peace—
transferring men to blessed Alaska—
the form neglected to state the number of men.
Ben added his name, Zacharias, last,
and flew into Anchorage.

No one discovered the ploy,
no one ordered him court-martialed
or, worse, shipped to Vietnam
to take eternal point on patrols;
no sniper made a shattered melon
of his head so not even his mother
could be sure she was grieving the right son;
no Bouncing Betty took his legs
like the snap of a T-Rex's jaws;
no VC exploded from a secret tunnel
and blasted him like a dummy
yanked backwards on a cord
for Saturday matinee amusement.

He typed and filed orders and memos;
on days off he hiked or cross-country skied,
once outran a blizzard descending a mountain
faster than a science-fiction cloud,
and swore it was the most thrilling thing
he'd ever done, except avoiding the war.

## OPEN HEART SURGERY

When he was a kid, surgeons cracked
Carl's chest open like a boiled crab
and performed magic on his heart;
as a teenager at Manhattan Beach,
he never took off his T-shirt,
and when girls asked why, he'd smirk,

"You'd faint," to their nervous giggles,
one daring to lift the cotton and reveal
the staple-stitches, tracing them
with a sexy fingernail, kissing the welts
and walking off, hand-in-hand with him.
I wanted to kill him for his luck.

At the army physical, 4-F, our hero,
even if as a kid his lips were the blue
of not enough oxygen
from his splintered-crystal heart.

"You're so lucky," I punched his arm,
days after the army doctor asserted
I was fit to fire a rifle, my right hand
more numb than a bucket of mud.

"Use your left," the quack pointed:
Vietnam ripping our hearts like Aztec priests
ensuring bountiful harvests.

Carl? The poor bastard's heart exploded
a week later, his lucky years over.

## COWARD

At a party in Maryland, where I was visiting
an old friend from our Brooklyn neighborhood,
a girl announced her fiancé was on R & R.
When I asked what that meant, she spat,

"Are you the stupidest human on the planet
or just being a snotty coward scared of Vietnam;
because if you really didn't believe in the war
you'd be freezing your ass off in godless Canada,
or rotting in prison, a conscientious objector;
or a non-combatant medic, saving the lives
of much better, braver men than you."

She had me, but I couldn't shut up:

"That's me, but this has to be the most idiotic,
pointless, murderous war ever devised by evil old men.
I hope your fiancé comes home whole and marries you
and you have lots of kids and live happily ever after,
but since the army kills its own, I won't hold my breath."

I would've flung more kerosene on the dancing flames,
tears grenading down her cheeks, but Stan dragged me out.

"You never know when to stop!" he accused.

"Drop me at the Greyhound station," I muttered.

"Don't be a jerk," he answered, trying for old time's sake
not to say a word, though he'd told me earlier
he'd be going in right after he finished medical school.

## MARTY BANNING ESCAPES VIETNAM

Marty was lucky, stationed in South Korea,
not that death-zone Pete Seeger called
"The Big Muddy." Just the crazy North
across DMZ razor-wire, a million soldiers
dying to invade or infiltrate for a tyrant's glory
or, as Phil Ochs sang,

"Guns will be guns, and boys will be boys."
Still, a board game, compared to Vietnam.

When he could forget both sides were poised
like monstrously armed football teams
before they explode with the snap,
Marty's big problem was which college
to attend after his hitch was up.

On leaves, he'd hop a deuce-and-a-half
into Seoul, and tell himself he loved
this one really cute bar girl; then, almost
in the blink of an eye, he was home

and realized he hadn't breathed in two years,
terrified he'd be transferred to Vietnam.

## DEMOLITION EXPERT, I

Theodore loved to blow things up:
his whiny sister's dolls,
his toy soldiers, the bigger
and bigger locks
on the barbwire fence
that kept us from playing
in the vacant lot
next to our apartment house.

Anything that made a boom,
a blinding flash, smelled of smoke
and splattered things sky high,
he was a hooked trout for.

We thought he'd grow up—
if he survived the explosions,
or the prison he was hurtling for
faster than a short dynamite fuse—
to be a nuclear physicist
or a demolitions expert.

Older, he volunteered his expertise;
the army straitjacketed him
as an infantryman in Vietnam.
He sent one letter home, then MIA,
the army informed his stunned parents.

But when the TV news showed
old buildings dominoed down
in a dust-spray of well-placed explosives,
or when I read articles about
bigger and better bombs going off
at ROTC headquarters, at companies
that made Napalm, or at munitions plants,
I wondered if Theodore hadn't snuck back
Stateside, and was working at what he loved.

## AT STATION ELEVEN

After my visit with the draft board,
I was invited to present to the army shrink
my psychiatrist's letter: making me out
to be crazier than Hamlet stabbing Polonius.
I sat, my leg piston-jerking hard enough to shoot
through a Fiat's hood, and saw the kid,
naked except for his briefs and Irish hair
wild as if he'd skipped rope with a live
electrical wire, as he sleepwalked the room.

"Fall in!" a doctor ordered in a voice
accustomed to being obeyed with
"Sir, yes, Sir!" terror. The kid ignored him.
"Fall in!" the doctor bellowed, not sure
if the kid was full of it or zombie-shuffling crazy.

When two MP's shouted similar commands,
again, nothing: one aimed his rifle at the kid's face,
blood about to paint the floor and walls,
when the kid launched everything he'd eaten
the past week all over the barrel;
all of us pivoted away, but silently cheered
a truly great performance,
the kid collapsing, carried out.

After I'd spoken to the army shrink
and was told I'd have to see yet one more shrink,
I saw "Red" dancing away. I ran after him,
to ask how he'd done it, but he'd vanished.

## THE ARMY REJECT

While I waited to convince
an army shrink I was too nuts to serve,
a kid stumbled out of his interview;
he slumped down, head in hands.

"Couldn't get out?" I wanted to be kind
through my own terror of the head doctor
who would shout I was a liar, a coward.

"They rejected me!" he wailed.
"I wanted to make my daddy proud."

Too easy to joke at his patriotic expense,
I wrapped an arm, like a prayer shawl,
around his shoulder while he sobbed,
more ashamed than if he'd gotten a girl
pregnant and then had sneered,

"You ain't nothing but a whore,"
knowing what she'd let him do
was out of love for him.

"The doc warned my heart could explode
any moment, but hell, I played football
in high school. What'll I tell my daddy?"

"That you did your best," I tried to sound
like an adult assuaging his teenage son's sorrows.
Then my name was called; I rose and walked
to the shrink's office, a dead man already.

"Good luck," the kid called out.
"I hope it goes better for you."

## HO, HO, HO CHI MINH

I never had the guts
to burn my draft card
in a public ceremony
captured by censorious media
and celebrated by granny-dressed,
colt-legged hippie-chicks
whose taunting mantra
to the cops was,

"Girls say yes for guys
who say no!"

On peace marches, we'd chant,

"Ho, Ho, Ho Chi Minh,
the NLF is gonna win!"

as if the National Liberation Front
was our Super Bowl favorite,
feeling, for the moment,
more radical and dangerous
than I knew I was.

## BEFORE A SCREENING OF *PLANET OF THE APES*

Years before I knew what a right-wing,
gun-crazed asshole Charlton Heston was,
and thought him merely more bombastic
than the board treaders Dickens satirized,
I decided to see *Planet of the Apes,*
nothing else playing, no band
at the Fillmore I wanted to hear.

Vietnam was raging like a dragon long
as the Mekong River, so the theatre owner piped in
"The National Anthem" before the movie.
I could've stood with everyone else,
placed my hand over my heart,
and pretended to belt out the lyrics.

But I sat, arms folded: Bad enough to rise
before a Mets game, though rich Yankee fans
hauled their girths up, to thank America
that someone else, someone poorer,
was willing to die for them.

"Show," a guy hissed, "some freakin' respect."

"What's your name, asshole," another
taunted, "Julius-Jew-Traitor-Rosenberg?"

That did it; I shot up and pointed a finger
in the guy's face and demanded,
"Why aren't you serving, Mr. Super Patriot?"
Lucky the entire audience didn't pound me
into the buttered-popcorn-sticky floor.

Instead, we all watched Heston chew
scenery like he hadn't eaten for weeks.

# PART III.
# WAR BUSINESS

"War's good business so give your son
and I'd rather have my country die for me."

—"rejoyce," Grace Slick

## DEMOLITION EXPERT, II

I met him on line to collect
unemployment benefits;
he was just back from Vietnam
and wore his "freak flag" in a bandana.
After we soul-brother shook,
he confided,

"I need a good six months rest
after the combat zone."

"They'll make you go out
on job interviews," I warned.

"Bro," he snickered,
"I was an explosives expert
in-country. How many jobs
you think there are for guys
like me in New York?

"I'll finally get some sleep
and smoke righteous weed
with these government checks,
which I figure is fair, after
what I went through, to be standing
here on my only two legs."

When I confessed the shrink's
bogus letter I was hoping
would save me, we slapped skin.

"I don't regret Indian Country,"
he whispered, "but if you can get out
by any means necessary,
do it, Bro."

## GO-BETWEENS

At this party, they were friends of friends,
on shore leave from submarine duty,
soon to ship back to Southeast Asia;
a euphemism for Vietnam, they shook
their resigned heads, sighed, apologizing
for being dragged into that lying swamp
of a war. Then they got down to business.

"Where can we score some lids, hash,
and psychedelics, to keep us sane?"

I was tempted to ask where,
in such a cramped space could they stash
all that shit, but decided they'd already
conquered that quartermaster problem.

We pulled out baggies, blotter strips, packets
of blond Lebanese hash—aromatic as chocolate—
gifts to two guys we'd just met to assuage our guilt
that they were doing our dirty work,
while I was trying to dig my way out
of the draft, like a terrified mouse.

## A SUNDAY PROMENADE

We were hemmed in by mounted cops
in helmets Mussolini might've worn,
as we tried to march on the U.N.
to protest the G.I.s and Vietnamese killed,

when what had been a Sunday promenade—
mothers with strollers, lovers arm in arm,
most of us shouting slogans
that *must* change the government's mind—

became a screaming stampede: mounted cops
clubbing everyone, young women's heads
blossoming blood, while we tried to shield them,
but knocked down by horses trained not to mind
jellyfish-squishy bodies under their hooves.

We ran, chased by a cop on horseback
as we flew down the stairs to the subway,
vaulted the turnstiles, and turned to see the cop
urging his mount to soar over those gates,
gallant as National Velvet taking a jump,
its rider forgetting the low-beamed ceiling.

## MICKEY MILLER

In high school, Mickey was the one kid
who didn't run like a panicked rabbit
from Tommy Lockhart and his wolves.
Instead, he waited for mad Tommy
to close in, swinging his fists, bellowing
like a berserker, spittle sharp as acid.

Mickey stood calm as swordsman
Toshiro Mifune in a samurai movie
and swung his stone-loaded sock,
Tommy going down like a hodful
of bricks dropped from a construction site.

Years later, a cop, Mickey patrolled
a peace march on horseback, funneling
us marchers away from the U.N.
Think of that apocryphal incident between
Thoreau and Emerson—Ralph Waldo
demanding of Henry David why he was in jail
for civil disobedience, Thoreau accusing,
"Why are you not?" That would've been
my question to Mickey about why
he wasn't protesting the Vietnam War.

I never had the chance to ask: Mickey
swinging his club like a knight's mace.
At the instant before he would've sent me
into star land, he stopped himself, and roared,

"Bobby, get the hell outta here!" then spurred
his mount on while I stood, shaking.

## POTATOES OR GRITS: WASHINGTON, D.C.

This was the peace march to end the War,
uncountable thousands descending
on D.C., though according to the cops
maybe fifteen die-hard malcontents showed up.
But we were, if not Sparactus' millions,
over 100,000, shouting, singing songs
Nixon would hear and dope-smack
his forehead and instantly stop the bombing,
the sending of boys like me into that hell-zone,
then beg forgiveness of the whole world.

We arrived the night before, were directed
to a church, to sing and sleep until we formed up
in the morning, when we rose early, found
a greasy spoon where I ordered eggs and toast:
marching and shouting slogans hungry work.

"Potatoes or grits?" the counterman demanded.

"What are grits?" I asked in my ignorance.

He shot me a killing glare of deciding
if I were a traitor or just stupid, and challenged,
"Boy, y'awl a Yankee?"

"Potatoes," I muttered, meaning I was indeed
a Yankee outside agitator in his peaceful capital,
and was all for the commie inspired civil rights
of shiftless blacks, only he'd have used the other word.

The plate crashed down in front of me;
I shoved in the food, paid, and with my friends
shooting me looks of "What the hell was that?"—
walked to the march site: mounted bulls
hemming in our multitudes just a little,
to let us know what could happen.

## AT THE PEACE MARCH: WASHINGTON, D.C., 1970

We walked five abreast past the White House,
police horses snorting in our faces, their hot
sides nudging us to stay in line, the mounts
trained not to flinch from sudden movements,
not to mind stepping on protestors, not to care
about our surging, shouting multitudes.

But George, my cousin Sammy's friend,
tried to break out of line and stab his penknife
into mounts' flanks, hoping we'd follow him
into a full-scale riot, our faces bloodied
by the forces of fascism on the late news.

"Are you trying to get us all killed?"
I finally yanked him by his collar.

"This is pointless," he flung off my grip.
"Anyone can march like robots. We need
to make war-loving Republican parents
see their kids getting manhandled by the Pigs."

Maybe he had a point; maybe he was all talk,
for when Sammy gave him a look of

"Stop it, asshole," George shrugged,
fell back in line, and marched
as peacefully as the rest of us.

## THE WORST THING THAT EVER HAPPENED
## AT A PEACE MARCH

We never got beaten or busted
and had to spend nights
in a makeshift stadium jail,
sleeping on a sleet-freezing field,
thrown slops, and denied
our one phone call.

But once, we lost my cousin
Sammy in the multitudes
that had poured into D.C.
to exorcise Nixon's bombs:
malevolent water balloons.
Sammy's wife, Laurel, panicked
when we reached the parking garage
and he wasn't there.

"Where's my husband?"
she demanded, as if we'd handed
him over to the cops or the FBI
for interrogation, torture,
experiments with drugs
that made acid feel like
a civilized glass of sherry.
We tried to convince her
Sammy knew where we were
and would find his way to us,
just give him time.

Finally he did,
hugging Laurel, apologizing
that the crowds were too thick,
so he'd waited, as if for the stragglers
in a cattle or buffalo stampede,
not rubbing the hickey
I noticed for the first time.

Several months later,
William was born; Sammy and Laurel
stayed together until war's end,
family men exempt.

## MY FATHER AT A PEACE RALLY, NEW YORK CITY

A conga line of Hare Krishnas
and war resisters in the Garment District
chanting, bopping to cymbals and drums,
when a construction worker sneered,

"Lookit them peace faggots; up to them,
we'd all be bowing to Uncle Joe Stalin
like he was Jesus' favorite son."
The guy he muttered to, my dad,
returning from lunch, the *Times*
crossword puzzle under his arm.

"How's it your business?" he barked.
The guy bellowed back with an attitude:

"I ain't broken no one's jaw today. Yet."

I was at my parents' for Friday supper,
and to watch the Knicks with my dad,
then ride the subway back to my apartment
and try not to worry, too much,
about the draft board's hot wolf-breath
freezing the back of my sweaty neck.

Dad was relishing the story after a shot
or two of rye, Mom wringing her hands,

"Sol, he could've killed you."

"That'll be the day," he chortled—a boxer
in his youth—and flicked off a blinking-quick
left-right to show how he'd have handled the guy
who'd called my dad "Commie lover,"
then shook his head at the state of the world.

"You got any of that marijuana anymore?"
Dad nudged me while we watched the Knicks.
When I could breathe again, I rolled him a joint
and wished like hell I'd seen him in his glory.

## AT A MEETING OF AN ANTI-WAR
## STEERING COMMITTEE

Because the meeting would end late at night,
which meant a treacherous subway ride home,
my friend Maddie asked me to join her, and pleaded,

"Please, Bob, don't say anything crazy."

So I sat, Maddie wearing her hair anarchist wild,
her granny glasses glittering anti-war passion,
while ideas were batted like dying shuttlecocks,
and I fought off yawning by raising a hand,
Maddie muttering, "Why can't you just sit still,"
so she could impress the guy in charge.

"You want Nixon's attention?" I drawled,
a young Brando rebelling against everything.
"Throw miniature footballs over the White House fence,
each pigskin painted: "Vietcong 49-Nixon 0."

Stunned silence; Maddie hid her head;
Roger, the guy she wanted to eat up, snarled,

"Are you fucking nuts? We throw anything
at the White House, we're mowed down by the Pigs!"

"Thank you so very much," Maddie fumed,
while we waited for the F Train home.
"Now I'm in cahoots with J. Edgar Hoover!"

"I'm sorry," I mumbled. "I don't know
what came over me." But I did, exactly.

## THE RADIO CALL-IN SHOW

The show pandered to the Moral Majority;
a buddy and I listened one night, snickering
at the callers who proclaimed we were winning,
and anyone who didn't believe that truth
of American greatness should go back to Russia.
So Fred called the show and lied he was a sergeant,
just returned from a tour of duty in Vietnam.

My heart sank for the guys who did serve
and came home in boxes or shattered.
But Fred claimed, blithe as Dennis the Menace,
that he'd witnessed atrocities, and anyone
who hadn't been there shouldn't declare us righteous.
I hid my head, as if the host were shouting, "Liar!"
But he just stammered apologies to Warrior Fred.

"Fred, please shut up," I muttered, afraid
the army could somehow find out Fred and I
were still crawling along a bayonet blade
to find a safe way out. But he spewed more crap
about his service, and after he hung up, he asserted,
over my stare dirtier than Mekong Delta mud,

"They deserved it, bunch of fascist hypocrites."

## 50,000

At one peace march, organizers handed out
black arm bands with white lettering: "50,000."
Immediately, a reporter blocked my path,
his microphone a drawn sword,

"What does that number stand for?"

This was years before Fox News decided
"Fair and Balanced" meant telling lies
to save their democracy. But even then,
a chunk of the media sold the mendacities
that the War defended our sacred way of life.

"The number of GIs killed in combat," I spat.
He stabbed at me again with his microphone:

"Why are you not helping the War effort?"
And maybe because I'd tried, and failed,
for Conscientious Objector status
and now was hoping for being crazy;
or maybe because, like Phil Ochs, I feared
the war might never end, I shot back,

"Why aren't you in Vietnam,
if you're so fucking patriotic?"

Peace marches getting more and more
like two enemy armies preparing for war.

## DRAFT NUMBERS

My brother's was 305;
a friend's 251; they didn't know
whether to laugh or cry in relief.

Another pal was dealt a number so low,
he decided, "Screw it," and enlisted
in the Marines: instead of Vietnam,
he was sent to be tested: freezing water,
heat, tanks of dark and silent madness;
doses of LSD to sizzle his brains:
to determine where discomfort ended
and torture began, but he never fired a rifle,
or ducked from an enemy's shell,
even with his number eighteen,
not close to the lucky Hebrew number.

In the Nineties, the right wing
gubernatorial candidate
of my adopted western state claimed
he'd forgotten his draft number.
Guys were more likely to forget anniversaries,
their beloved wives' birthdays.

## FINAL INTERVIEW
## WITH AN ARMY PSYCHIATRIST

The third time I was summoned
to Kafka's (or rather, Dracula's) Castle
at Fort Hamilton, I didn't shave, shower,
or change my clothes for three weeks,
so the shrink couldn't see, or smell,
how sane I was, compared to guys
nuttier than a can of cashews.

My leg jerked like a trout desperate
against the hook, not a sound squeaking
through the doctor's door:
more frightening than if he'd shouted
at the kid ahead of me. Finally, Dr. Bernstein
spat in an accent more Himmler than Elie Wiesel,

"Your letter says you are homosexual,"
he smelled a lie. "Do you sleep
with your roommate?" and waited for me
to betray myself as incompetently hetero
in an era when gays in the army
were run away from with the terror
of a lady in a Marx Brothers movie
shrieking at a mouse. Inspiration
alighted like Athena's owl.

"He's too fat." Oh the blessed shrink shouting,

"4-F! Get out!" I floated the miles
to my parents' apartment, the sun warm
and healing as the first of May.

"Bobby?" my mother's voice
the hope of seeing Grandpa rise from the dead.

"Hi Mom." I tried to sound nonchalant
as Willie Mays making a basket catch.

We hugged, circled an impromptu hora,
until we collapsed into happy tears.
We're hugging still, when I dream of her alive.

# PART IV.
# "I DECLARE THE WAR IS OVER."

—Phil Ochs

## AUGUST 9, 1974: THE DAY NIXON RESIGNED

Free of the clutching, clawing draft,
I'd moved to Denver for grad school,
and was strolling downtown
when I saw the newspaper headline,

"NIXON RESIGNS"

to send me reeling into a rage
of kicking at the machine:
that the lying, thieving, murderous
son of a bitch who'd cheated
his way into the Presidency

hadn't been indicted, sentenced,
dragged through the streets, hanged,
his corpse tormented like Mussolini's,
when Italians had shouted,

"Basta! Enough!"

I was gathering myself to kick again,
when a little old lady gripped my arm,
and in a schoolmarm
creaky voice, admonished,

"Young man, vandalism is not how
we vent our frustration. Even on him,"
she pointed as if at a dead rat.

## THE DECENCY

After Nixon was forced to resign,
Professor Stanley spat—
while he treated a bunch of us
grad students to Friday afternoon beers—

"If only he'd had the decency
to blow his brains out."

Professor Stanley had flown missions
over Korea, where, it was rumored,
he'd once bombed the wrong village.

More rumors had it he'd tried to kill himself,
but the gun was wrestled from his grip,
and years of counseling had helped.

We padded past his sobbing office
that late Friday afternoon, a couple
of us grad students bull-shitting
down the hall in our own cubby-hole office:

until he knocked, and asked
if he could treat us all to a few beers,
and we thought it a kindness
not to let him drink alone.

## ELEGY FOR PHIL OCHS

After Dylan went electric, surrealistic,
Phil Ochs was the one protest folksinger
who used plain, angry English in
"I Ain't Marching Anymore,"
and "I Declare the War Is Over,"
when it seemed Vietnam would drag on
until it killed every kid in the country.

But the War finally did end,
and no one heard from Ochs for years;
then one morning, a newspaper interview;
confiding he'd nothing left to say,
no cause he could ride to the rescue of,
plus a hint of a drinking problem,
of disappointment he hadn't been a bigger star.

Years later, I read a biography of him:
in his final months, Mr. Hyde staggering
around the Bowery, turning up to sleep
for a night or two on terrified friends' couches,
and threatening to kill people,
his eyes wild as Spencer Tracy playing
Dr. Jekyll's murder-mad alter ego.

Finally, his teenage nephew found Ochs
hanging from a kitchen beam: the kid maybe
thinking—before he got home from school—
of a snack, of calling a girl he couldn't stop
dreaming about, of shooting hoops,
and maybe even doing his homework,

while Ochs twisted and the rope creaked,
the only music, the one protest, left to him.

## WATCHING PRESIDENT JOHNSON ANNOUNCE
## HE WOULDN'T RUN

Rather than the mad-wolf murderer
of President Kennedy, of Martin Luther King,
of thousands of boys duped into dying in Asia,
and even more butchered Vietnamese,

I remember a bloodhound that's given up
on the scent in a swamp that will drown it:
a man beaten down by the office, by the war
that had no end except in an open grave
that might swallow the whole world,
a man who'd be dead soon after his term was up.

He was swearing he'd not accept the nomination,
would not serve, wanted only to rid himself
of being blamed for everything by everyone;
all he wanted, a little quiet, to hear the Texas
hill-country wind twang sad country-
western songs of lost love.

That's what I think now; back then, we cheered
to drive a stake into the vampire's heart,
that we could end Vietnam in a few minutes.
Instead, Nixon gave us more years of war, of lies,
of deaths piling up like logs shipped by water
and clogging the currents at the bends of rivers.

But for the moment we saw only the beaten despot,
the slain monster we'd compared to regicide-Macbeth,
though it tugs at my heart now, that he looked
frail as my exhausted father that Sunday I visited
him and my mother, to eat dinner, watch football,
crack jokes, then ride the subway home.

Dad too tired to walk me to the door,
I'd bent and kissed him, not a thought in my head
that it would be for the last time.

## MAY HIS NAME BE WRITTEN

With my wife at a revival of *Hair,*
I remembered that old friend who'd tried
to hand me a blank check to escape Vietnam.

"Go to Canada," he'd folded the paper
into my fist, but I was too afraid
to take that one step beyond the border
of what middle class boys did and didn't do.
So I'd thanked him, and though I didn't go in,
we soon lost contact, and forgot each other.

But watching young actors strut, dance,
and sing of the Age of Aquarius, Vietnam,
and the draft, it was crucial to thank him.

The next day, Beth found his email address,
and I wrote, reminded him of his attempt
to save my life, told him I didn't expect
to hear from him, but wanted to thank him,
even if forty ungracious years too late.

The next day, an email: he confided
he hadn't thought of that night since then.

More important, his wife had just died,
and he'd not wanted to live any longer,
but my message had given him hope.

So—he concluded—we were even.

## SOME OF THE ABLES ON THE WALL

Among the far too many boys and men
who left their only lives in Vietnam,
just the ghosts of their names returned again:
like the Ables, carved into the Wall's calm

and cool-dark stone: Bobby Lee, Charles Edward,
David Anthony, Frank Wayne, Jim Farrell,
and more of that family: scattered shards
of the Ables, dead in a jungle hell.

Not one of them able to leave the Wall,
but pinned like butterflies there, for all time,
their names frozen by printing, neat and small
to last long as hard stone, longer than rhyme.

Small comfort to be carved in silent black,
no Ables able to get their lives back.

## GUYS MY AGE

I see them on the street in their wheelchairs,
guys my age, their gray hair in ponytails,
American flags taped to their rear handles.

In summer their T-shirts might read,
"I know I'm going to Heaven,
because I served my time in Hell."

They're the ones who went to Nam,
believing the lies Johnson, then Nixon, spewed
like volcanic ash; or not having a choice

against the draft's giant lava flow
that swept them away on a killing current.
They came home in pieces, given wheelchairs.

This guy's chair is motorized;
it looks like the latest model, almost
something you might ride for fun.

I've drifted into the crosswalk
in my hurry to finish my morning errands,
then drive home for lunch.

Seeing him, I back up, so he won't
have to swerve into oncoming traffic.
As he whirs past, he nods in thanks

for my courtesy. I nod back, the least
I can do for him, who every day
of his life lives the war I dodged.

## ACKNOWLEDGMENTS

The author wishes to thank the editors of the following journals, where these poems, some in earlier form and with slightly different titles, first appeared:

*Dead Snakes Review:* "At the Peace March: Washington, D.C., 1970," "The Worst Thing That Ever Happened at a Peace March, March, 1970," "At Station Eleven"
*The Homestead Review:* "The Decency"
*Iodine Poetry Journal:* "Super Bowl III, January 12, 1969"
*Misfit Magazine:* "Demolition Expert, II," "50,000"
*New Orphic Review:* "Physical, Fort Hamilton," "The Shrink's Letter," "At the Draft Board, I," "At the Draft Board, II"
*Poetry Depth Quarterly:* "1969"
*Red Rock Review:* "Coward," "Marty Banning Escapes Vietnam"

*Cover artwork by Michael Welply and Roscoe Welply; author photo by Beth Cooperman; cover execution and interior book design by Diane Kistner; Avenir text and Copperplate titling*

## ABOUT FUTURECYCLE PRESS

FutureCycle Press is dedicated to publishing lasting English-language poetry books, chapbooks, and anthologies in both print-on-demand and Kindle ebook formats. Founded in 2007 by long-time independent editor/publishers and partners Diane Kistner and Robert S. King, the press incorporated as a nonprofit in 2012. A number of our editors are distinguished poets and writers in their own right, and we have been actively involved in the small press movement going back to the early seventies.

The FutureCycle Poetry Book Prize and honorarium is awarded annually for the best full-length volume of poetry we publish in a calendar year. Introduced in 2013, our Good Works projects are anthologies devoted to issues of universal significance, with all proceeds donated to a related worthy cause. Our Selected Poems series highlights contemporary poets with a substantial body of work to their credit; with this series we strive to resurrect work that has had limited distribution and is now out of print.

We are dedicated to giving all of the authors we publish the care their work deserves, making our catalog of titles the most diverse and distinguished it can be, and paying forward any earnings to fund more great books.

We've learned a few things about independent publishing over the years. We've also evolved a unique, resilient publishing model that allows us to focus mainly on vetting and preserving for posterity poetry collections of exceptional quality without becoming overwhelmed with bookkeeping and mailing, fundraising activities, or taxing editorial and production "bubbles." To find out more, come see us at www.futurecycle.org.

## THE FUTURECYCLE POETRY BOOK PRIZE

All full-length volumes of poetry published by FutureCycle Press in a given calendar year are considered for the annual FutureCycle Poetry Book Prize. This allows us to consider each submission on its own merits, outside of the context of a contest. Too, the judges see the finished book, which will have benefitted from the beautiful book design and strong editorial gloss we are famous for.

The book ranked the best in judging is announced as the prize-winner in the subsequent year. There is no fixed monetary award; instead, the winning poet receives an honorarium of 20% of the total net royalties from all poetry books and chapbooks the press sold online in the year the winning book was published. The winner is also accorded the honor of being on the panel of judges for the next year's competition; all judges receive copies of all contending books to keep for their personal library.

www.ingramcontent.com/pod-product-compliance
Lightning Source LLC
Chambersburg PA
CBHW070009100426
42741CB00012B/3175